Using Office 365

With Windows 8

Kevin Wilson

Apress®

Using Office 365: With Windows 8

Copyright © 2014 by Kevin Wilson

ISBN-13 (pbk): 978-1-4302-6685-3

ISBN-13 (electronic): 978-1-4302-6686-0

Compositor: SPi Global
Indexer: SPi Global
Artist: SPi Global
Cover Designer: Anna Ishchenko

Distributed to the book trade worldwide by Springer Science+Business Media New York, 233 Spring Street, 6th Floor, New York, NY 10013. Phone 1-800-SPRINGER, fax (201) 348-4505, e-mail orders-ny@springer-sbm.com, or visit www.springeronline.com. Apress Media, LLC is a California LLC and the sole member (owner) is Springer Science + Business Media Finance Inc (SSBM Finance Inc). SSBM Finance Inc is a **Delaware** corporation.

For information on translations, please e-mail rights@apress.com, or visit www.apress.com.

Apress and friends of ED books may be purchased in bulk for academic, corporate, or promotional use. eBook versions and licenses are also available for most titles. For more information, reference our Special Bulk Sales–eBook Licensing web page at www.apress.com/bulk-sales.

Any source code or other supplementary materials referenced by the author in this text is available to readers at www.apress.com. For detailed information about how to locate your book's source code, go to www.apress.com/source-code/.

Contents at a Glance

About the Author

Kevin Wilson, a practicing computer engineer and tutor, has had a passion for gadgets, cameras, computers, and technology for many years.

He graduated with masters degrees in computer science, software engineering, and multimedia systems. He has gone on to work within the computer industry, supporting and working with many different types of computer systems, as well as working within the educational system, running specialist lessons on filmmaking and visual effects for young people. He has also worked as an IT tutor, has taught in colleges in South Africa, and served as a tutor for adult education in England.

He continues to write books in the hope that his work will help people use their computers with greater understanding, productivity, and efficiency. His ultimate goal is to help students and people in countries, like South Africa, who have never used a computer before. It is his hope that they will, one day, get the same benefits from computer technology as we do.

Acknowledgments

Thanks to all the staff at Apress for their passion, dedication, and hard work in the preparation and production of this book.

To all my friends and family for their continued support and encouragement in all my writing projects.

To all my colleagues, students, and testers who took the time to test procedures and offer feedback on the book.

Finally, thanks to you, the reader, for choosing this book. I hope it helps you use your computer with greater ease.

Introduction

Using Office 365 introduces you to the new verson of Microsoft Office and is designed to help beginners and enthusiast users who want to get up and running quickly using their computers.

This book has been written in a step-by-step fashion, using photography and screen shots to illustrate the steps as clearly and concisely as possible. Starting with the fundamentals of what Office 365 is, we explore setting up your account, and learn about SkyDrive and SkyDrive Pro. We also take a look at the most common Office applications, with guided tutorials on creating documents in Word with different fonts, graphics, photographs, and colors. We learn how to manipulate data in Excel to create tables, perform calculations, and create charts. We use PowerPoint to get our message across by creating multimedia presentations using graphics, photograhs, and animations. We also learn how to set up Outlook to check our e-mail and keep appointments and contacts. Finally, we discover how to store documents with SkyDrive and SkyDrive Pro, and collaborate and share documents, presentations, and spreadsheets with friends and colleagues.

CHAPTER 1

■ ■ ■

Microsoft Office 365

Microsoft Office 365 is a subscription-based version of Microsoft Office 2013. Unlike any of the traditional Office suites such as Office 2010, Office 365 allows you to install Office applications on up to five different PCs and Macs, plus five mobile devices. With an Office 365 subscription, you can upgrade to the latest versions of Office for free.

In addition to the latest Office applications, your subscription includes some additional features, such as Office on Demand, 20 GB of additional online storage space through SkyDrive, and the option to install Office 2011 on Mac computers.

Let's review some of the features now.

Office on Demand

With Office on Demand, you can stream full versions of the following applications temporarily to another computer.

Office on Demand

 Word document

 Excel workbook

 PowerPoint presentation

 Access database

This comes in handy if you need to edit Office files on a computer that does not have Office installed. Simply go to www.office.com and sign in with your Microsoft Account ID and under "Office on Demand" you will see links to some office Applications such as Word, Excel, Powerpoint and Access. To launch the application, click on the link.

You will then see the application load up as shown in the following screen.

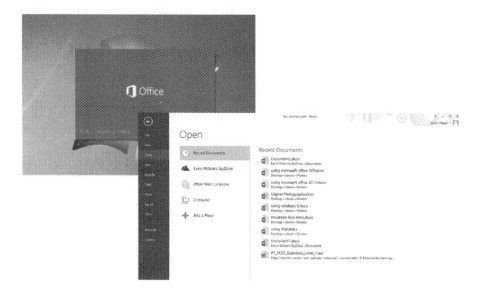

Office Web Apps

Office Web Apps allow you to run basic, cut-down versions of Office apps, such as Word, within your web browser as shown here.

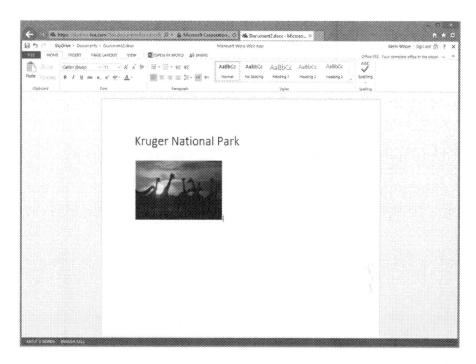

All your edited documents are stored on your SkyDrive and can be accessed from your account page on www.office.com.

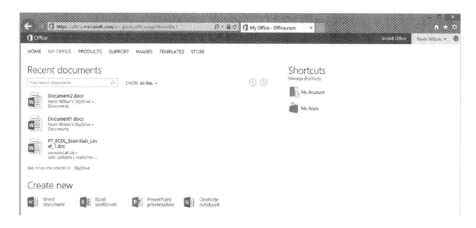

SkyDrive and SkyDrive Pro

SkyDrive comes in two versions, Sky Drive and SkyDrive Pro.

SkyDrive is aimed at consumers and ordinary home users. This is the version you would see if you signed up with Office 365 Home Premium. It allows you to save documents, photos, and other files on your SkyDrive. You can also share them with friends, and collaborate on content.

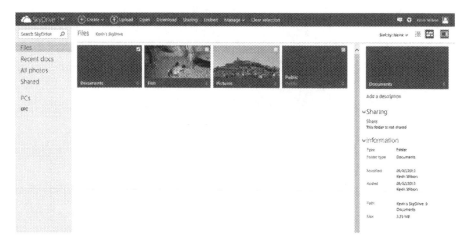

Alternatively, SkyDrive Pro is aimed at corporate and business users. It provides much the same experience as consumer SkyDrive, but includes additional functionality for IT administrators. For example, while overseeing a company's network, administrators can manage the SkyDrive Pro libraries and files by defining security, content policies, and more. SkyDrive Pro lets you share and collaborate on work documents with colleagues.

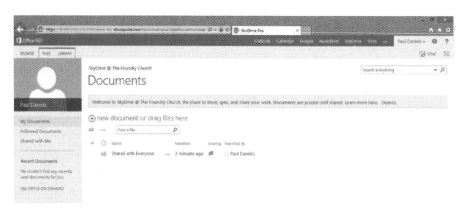

Most Used Office Applications

Microsoft Office 365 comes with a variety of applications. I have included the icons and the names of the applications here to make them easy to identify quickly.

Excel   OneNote   Outlook   Word   PowerPoint

Access   Publisher

We will be concentrating on the most used applications in this book: Word, Excel, PowerPoint, and Outlook.

Microsoft Word

Microsoft Word is a word-processing program used for typing documents and desktop publishing. You can create letters, documents, cards, and more with it.

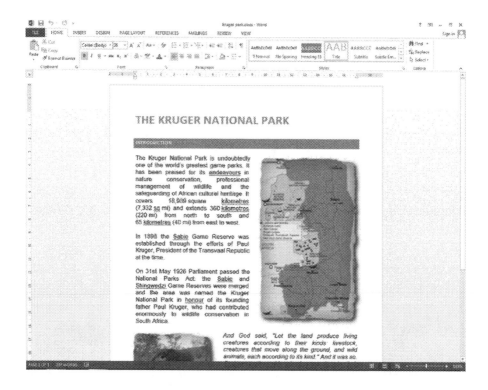

Microsoft Excel

Microsoft Excel is a spreadsheet program, used for organizing and analyzing financial data. You can create budgets, score sheets, and various data charts with it.

Microsoft PowerPoint

Microsoft PowerPoint is used for creating and giving presentations. It is used to create slideshows, using text and graphics, which can be displayed on-screen or shown to an audience using a projector.

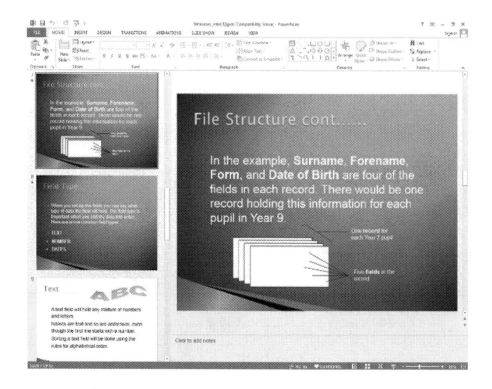

Microsoft Outlook

Microsoft Outlook is a personal information manager and e-mail system. It allows you to send and receive e-mails, as well as allowing you to keep address books of contacts and record appointments on an electronic calendar.

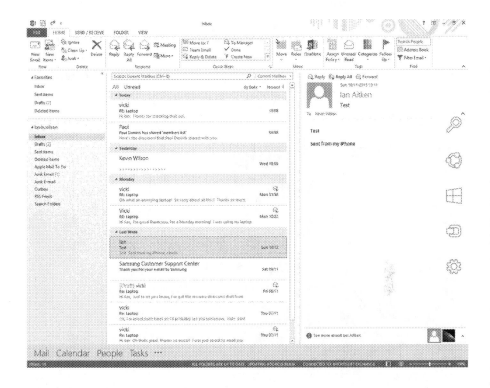

Other Applications

Microsoft OneNote is a note-taking and information-gathering application used with both tablet and conventional PCs. It gathers users' notes (handwritten or typed), drawings, screen clippings, and audio commentaries.

Microsoft Access is a database management system for keeping records.

Microsoft Publisher is a desktop publishing application used for creating brochures, flyers, and more. It differs from Microsoft Word in that the emphasis is placed on page layout and design rather than text composition and proofing.

In this book, we will be concentrating on the most widely used applications: Word, PowerPoint, Excel, and Outlook, as well as the SkyDrive app.

Creating a Microsoft Account

If you don't already have one, you'll need to create a Microsoft account in order to purchase Office 365. To do so, go to www.skydrive.com and follow these easy steps.

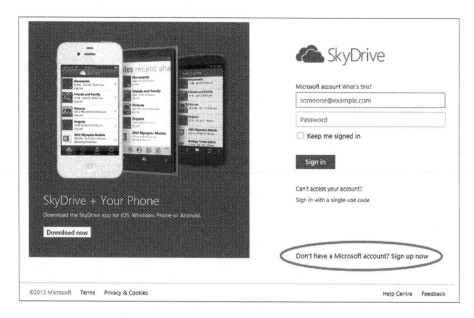

Click the "Sign up now" link on the bottom right of the screen.

You will see a form asking for your details. Fill it in and click the "I accept" button.

Once you have your Microsoft account, you can sign in using the same web site. This Microsoft account also gives you access to the App Store where you can purchase your Office apps, such as Office 365 Home Premium.

Installing Office

To install the Microsoft Office Suite, open your web browser, and sign in to Office 365 (www.office.com) with your Microsoft account on the machine you want to install office onto.

Go to your name on the top right and select "My account" from the drop-down list.

On the account page, you can see the number of installs available. Click the "Install" button to download and install Office on your computer.

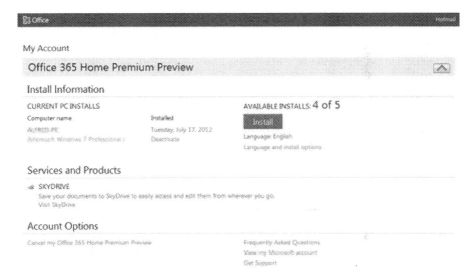

If this section is blank, click the link to "visit store to purchase your Office Apps."

After the install is complete, open an Office app such as Word, and click on a blank document.

Click "File," then click "Account" on the left-hand side, and select "Sign out."

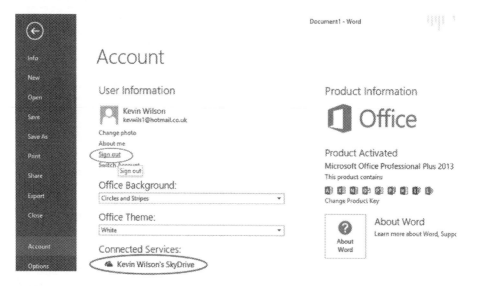

This will allow the next person to sign in with their own Microsoft account, rather than using yours.

Managing Account Settings

Because Office 365 is paid by either an annual or monthly subscription fee, you'll need to be able to manage your account settings, including payment information.

Go to www.office.com, then click the "Sign in" link at the top right-hand side of the page, and then enter your Microsoft Account ID and password.

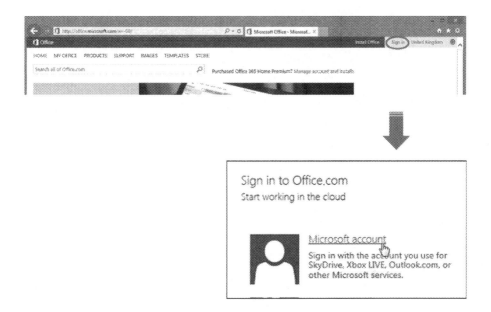

After you have signed in to your account, you will see your main screen (My Office page). From here, you can create new documents using the web app version of Office, or Office on Demand if you are using a computer that doesn't have Office installed locally.

All your documents currently on your SkyDrive are displayed here. Click "See more documents in SkyDrive" to view all your files on SkyDrive.

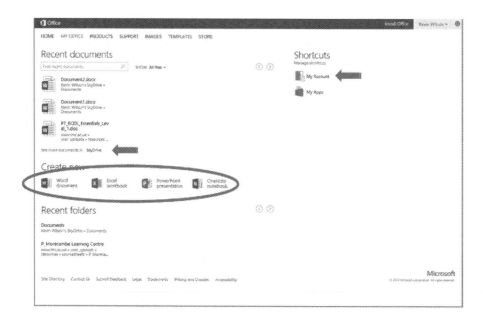

Clicking the icons shown under the "Create new" heading opens up a blank file in a web app or Office on Demand.

From the "My Account" link, you can manage subscriptions or buy more apps by purchasing them in the App Store.

CHAPTER 2

■ ■ ■

Microsoft SkyDrive and SkyDrive Pro

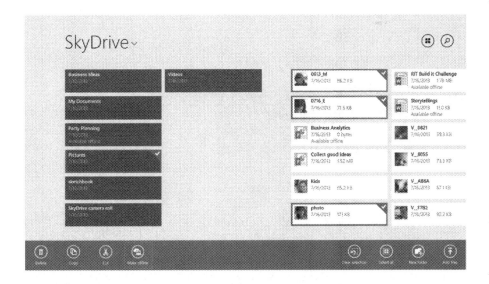

There are two versions of SkyDrive: SkyDrive and SkyDrive Pro.

SkyDrive is an online (cloud) storage area you can use as your own personal online hard drive. It is geared toward consumers and ordinary home users. When you create a document with one of the Office Web Apps, it will be saved to your SkyDrive. You can store other files there too, such as photos.

Both SkyDrive and Office Web Apps are located in the cloud, so they can be accessed with any device that has an Internet connection.

Alternatively, SkyDrive Pro (see later in chapter), is aimed at corporate and business users. It provides much the same experience as consumer SkyDrive, but includes additional functionality for IT administrators. For example, while overseeing a company's network, administrators can manage the SkyDrive Pro libraries and files by defining security, content policies, and more. SkyDrive Pro lets you share and collaborate on work documents with colleagues.

Getting Started with SkyDrive

You can access your SkyDrive online by logging in with your Microsoft account at www.skydrive.com.

You can switch between SkyDrive, e-mail, calendar by clicking here

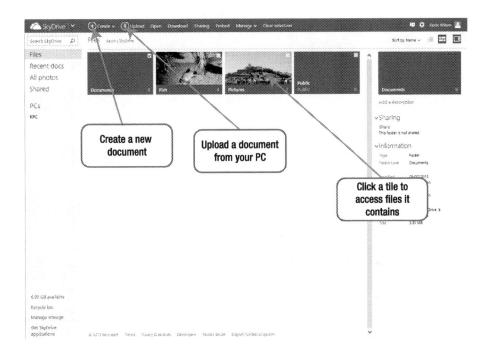

Creating a Document

Once SkyDrive is accessed, you can create a new document by clicking on the "Create" drop-down arrow and selecting the document of your choice. For example, in the following screen, I selected "Word document."

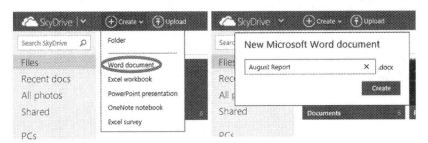

This will open a Word document in an Office Web App where you can edit your document and then save it to your SkyDrive.

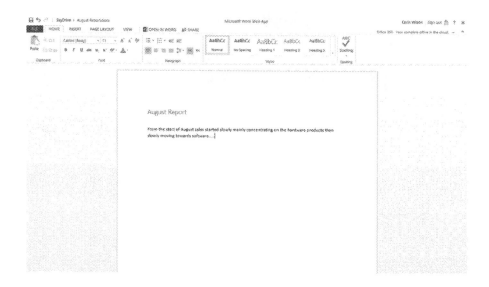

Sharing a Document

To share documents with someone, click the top right of the tile representing the document you want to share. This adds a check mark to the box, which means it has been selected. Once you have done that, click "Sharing" from the top menu.

Fill in the details of the recipient's Microsoft account e-mail address. The recipient can log in to their Microsoft account and begin editing the document.

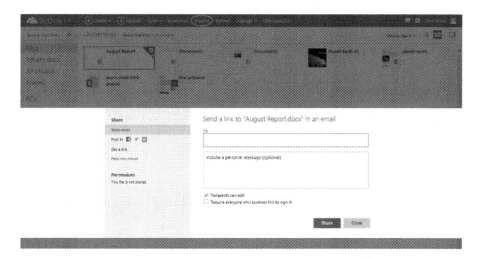

When more than one person is editing the document, you will see small icons next to paragraphs indicating that someone is editing that part of the document, as in the next screen.

Using SkyDrive App

The SkyDrive app is a useful feature if you are working on a PC, as it allows you to drag and drop files to your SkyDrive using your File Explorer, just as if you were moving files to another folder or drive on your computer.

To download it, go to "PCs" on the left side of your screen and click "Download SkyDrive for Windows."

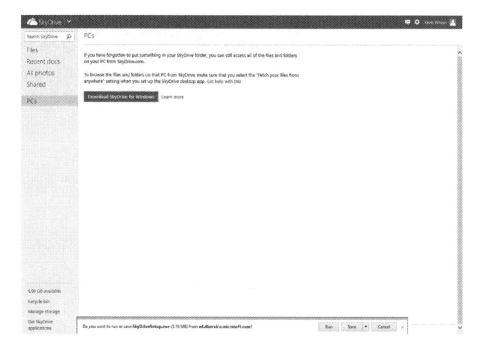

From the prompt that appears, select "Run." Then follow the instructions.

Click the "Get started" button and enter your Microsoft account e-mail and password.

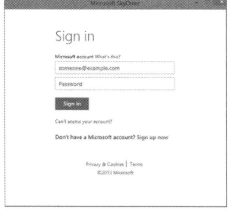

After SkyDrive is installed and you have signed in, you can find SkyDrive by going to your File Explorer on the desktop, as shown in the next image.

Uploading Files from Your Computer

Uploading files from your PC can be done using the Windows File Explorer.

Locate the file on your computer that you wish to upload to your SkyDrive using Windows File Explorer; in this case, the file I want is located in the Documents library.

Simply click and drag the file to the SkyDrive folder, as shown in the following screen.

You can also upload entire folders at once by dragging them to the SkyDrive folder in the same manner as uploading a single file.

Uploading Files on the Web

This can be useful if you are on a computer that doesn't have the SkyDrive app or the same version of Office as you have. You can upload files by signing in to your SkyDrive account at www.skydrive.com.

On your home screen, click "Upload," and in the dialog box that appears select the files you want to upload. In this case, I chose the Food Chain.doc file. To select multiple files, hold down the Ctrl key while you select your files.

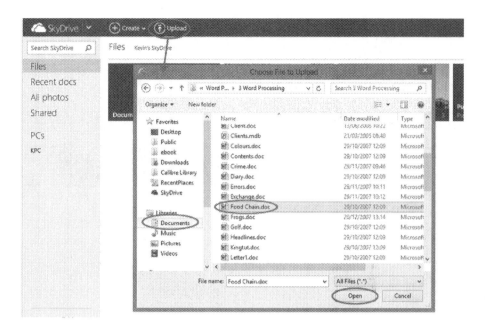

Once uploaded, it will appear on your home screen. You can also drag and
drop the file into a folder.

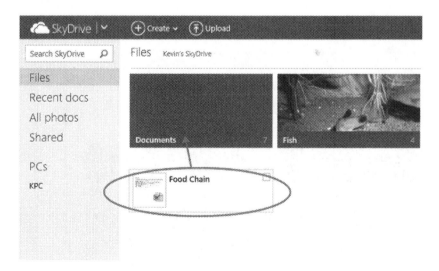

Checking Your E-mail

To check your e-mail, click on the drop-down arrow next to the SkyDrive icon on the top left of the screen.

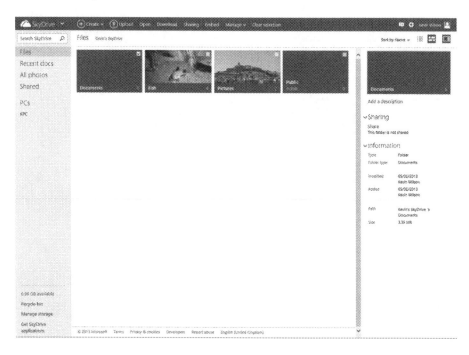

From the ribbon that appears, select Outlook.com.

From here, you can write a new e-mail by clicking "New," or read and reply to e-mails by clicking on the mail item in the list.

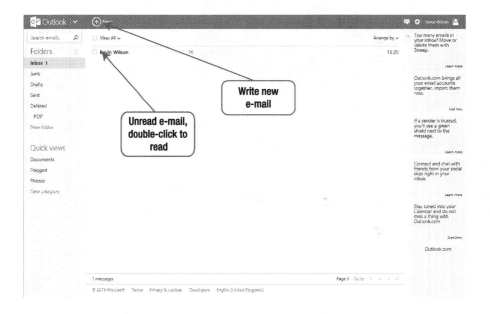

Getting Started with SkyDrive Pro

If an employer provided you with an e-mail address or Office 365 account, or you attend a college or university, you will likely be using SkyDrive Pro.

At the time of writing, you get 20 GB of storage space for your files. You access your account by going to portal.microsoftonline.com, then entering your e-mail address and password for your Office 365 account, given to you by your company, college, or other entity.

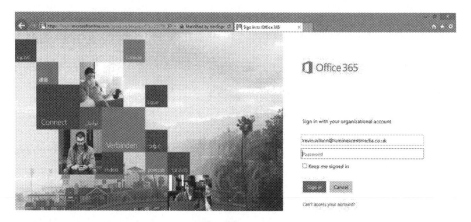

Following is your home screen when you have signed in to Office 365 on the web using your web browser. From here, you can check your e-mail, view or edit your files, and share documents.

To start using SkyDrive Pro, click on the SkyDrive icon on the top right of the menu bar, as shown in the following screen.

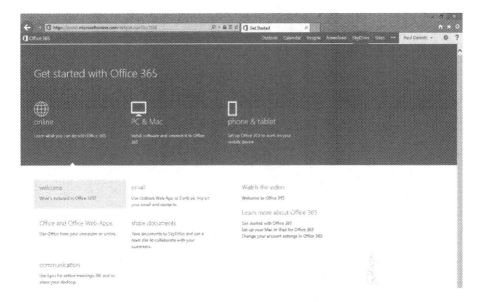

If this is the first time you have clicked this, Office 365 will take a few moments to set up your account.

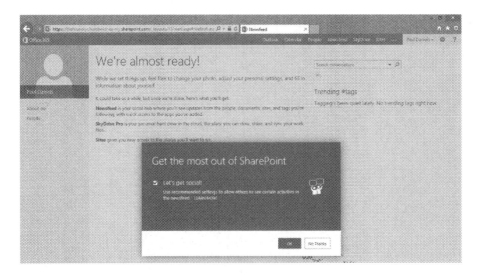

After it has finished, you will see your main screen, as shown in the next screen. From here, you can create new documents, share documents, and edit them.

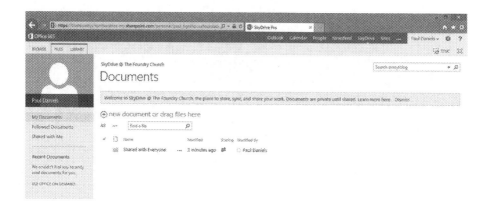

Creating a Document

To create documents using the web portal of SkyDrive Pro click on "new document" and select the type of file you want to create. This could be an Excel spreadsheet, a PowerPoint presentation, or a Word document. In this example, I am going to use a Word document.

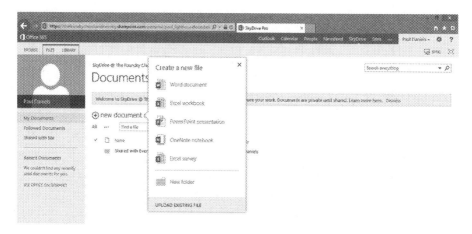

Give your document a meaningful name. Since mine is a list of members, I am going to call it "members list."

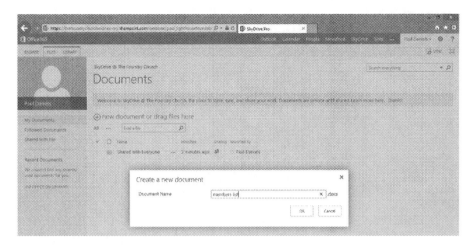

From here, you can edit your document on the web as if it were in Microsoft Word on your computer.

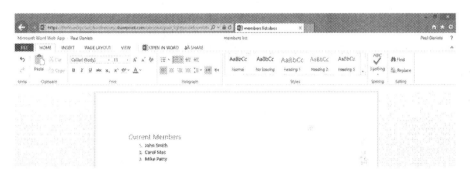

If you have Microsoft Word 2013 installed on your computer, you can click "Open in Word" to edit the document.

Sharing a Document

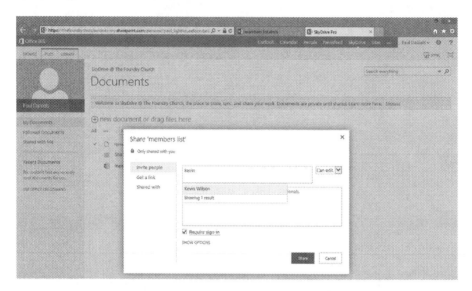

Following is the e-mail sent to Kevin Wilson.

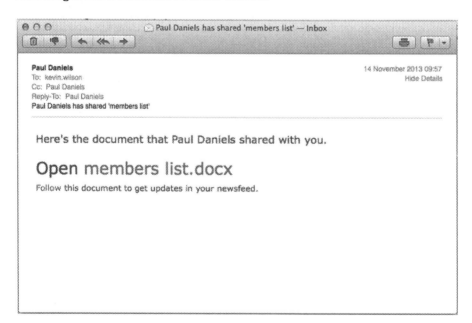

When Kevin Wilson opens the document, Word Web App will show the collaboration between the users. As you can see in the following screen, both Paul and Kevin are working on different sections of the document.

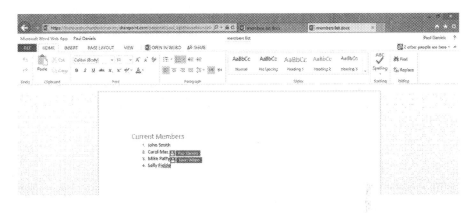

Uploading Files on the Web

You can upload the file by signing in to your SkyDrive account at portal.microsoftonline.com.

On your home screen, select "SkyDrive" from the menu along the top of the screen.

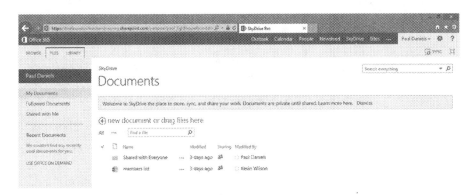

Click "Files," and in the menu tab that appears, select "Upload Document."

To select multiple files, hold down the Ctrl key while you select your files.

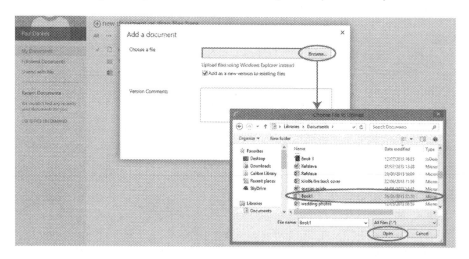

Once uploaded, it will appear on your home screen. You can also drag and drop the file into a folder.

You can now edit this document online anywhere using Office on Demand, Office Web Apps, or even a Microsoft Office application installed on another PC or device.

Checking Your E-mail

After you are signed in to your account using portal.microsoftonline.com, you can check your e-mail by clicking on the Outlook link on the top of the menu bar, as shown in the following screen.

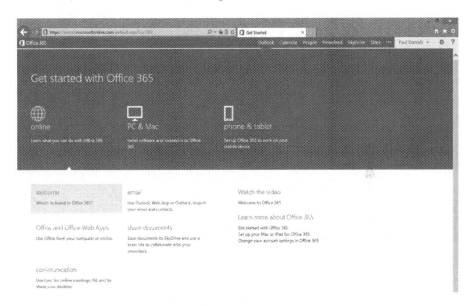

This will take you to Outlook's main screen.

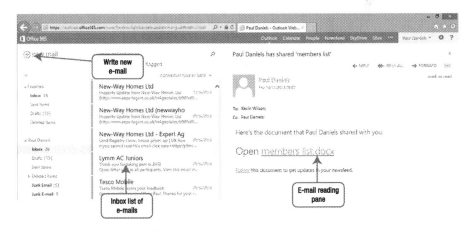

From here you can write a new e-mail by clicking "new mail," or you can read any of your e-mails in the inbox list by clicking on them. The e-mail you click on will be shown in the e-mail reading pane. From here, click reply to compose a reply to the e-mail.

CHAPTER 3

■ ■ ■

Microsoft Word 2013

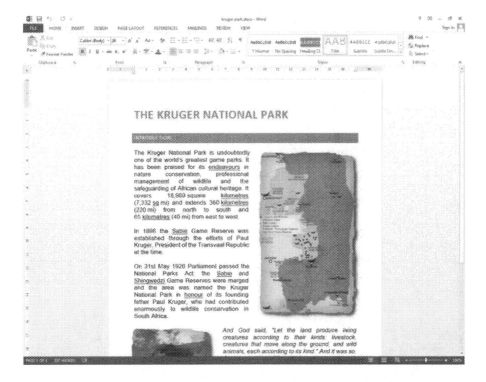

Microsoft Word allows you to create many different types of documents, from letters and resumes/CVs, to greetings cards, posters, and more.

Starting Word

To launch Word, go to the Start screen and select "Word 2013."

After Word has loaded, you can select a document from a wide variety of templates, such as brochures, CVs, letters, flyers, and more. If you want to create your own, just select the "Blank document." Your recently saved documents are shown in the blue pane on the left-hand side of the screen.

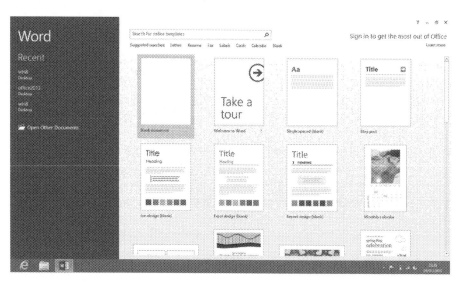

You can also search for a particular template using the search field at the top of the screen.

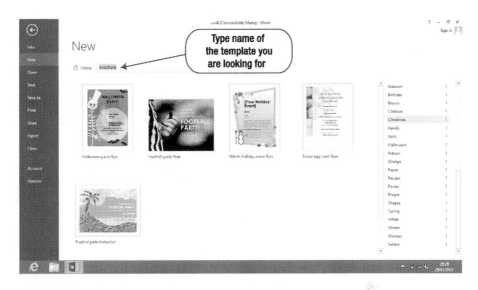

After you select a template, you will see your main work screen.

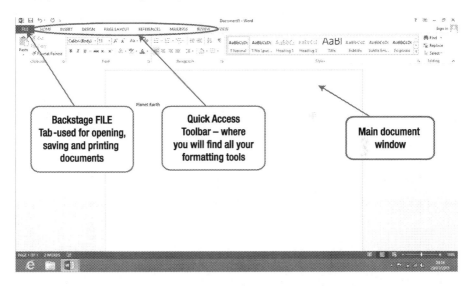

The Ribbon

All the tools used in Microsoft Word are organized on the Ribbon into tabs, loosely based on their function.

The most used tabs are, HOME, INSERT, and PAGE LAYOUT. For normal use of Word, these are the ones you will be using the most.

The HOME Tab

You will find your text-formatting tools here for making text bold, changing the style, font, paragraph alignment, and more.

The INSERT Tab

This is where you will find your clipart, tables, pictures, page breaks, and pretty much anything you would want to insert into a document.

The DESIGN Tab

Here is where you will find anything to do with preset themes and formatting, such as headings, colors, and fonts that you can apply to your document. Word can also automatically format your document according to the themes available.

The PAGE LAYOUT Tab

On this tab, you will find your page sizes, margins, page orientation (landscape or portrait), and anything to do with how your page is layed out.

Basic Text Formatting

When you first open a new document, it looks very plain. We need to format it.

Formatting is done primarily from the HOME tab.

Formatting Tools

Formatting tools are on the HOME tab, shown next.

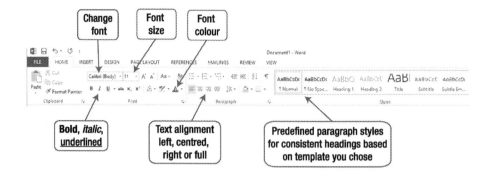

We can change the **font**, the size of the text, whether it is **bold**, *italic*, or underlined.

We can also change the alignment of the text to left aligned, centered, right aligned, or fully justified. Following is an example of fully justified text

Fully justified means it's aligned with both the left and right margins at the same time, which can make paragraphs of text look neater. It only really works on paragraphs like this, so you can see the left and right margins are both in line.

We can even change the color of the text. Maybe a bright red? Or perhaps a nice blue?

Predefined Styles

To format our document, we are going to use the predefined styles.

These are styles that have been already created to allow you to keep consistent-looking headings and text effects in your documents. They also make it easier to apply different font styles and sizes without having to set each individually every time.

So to change the text "Planet Earth" to Title style, highlight the title in your document as shown here.

Next, go to the Styles group in your HOME tab, and click the Title style choice, as shown below.

If I wanted to change the last paragraph to **bold**, I can select the whole paragraph and click the bold button in the Font group of the HOME tab.

Copy, Cut, and Paste

To ease editing documents, you can use copy, cut, and paste to move paragraphs or pictures around in different parts of your document. For example, in the document shown in the following screen I want to move the second paragraph after the image instead of before it. Simply cut and paste to do this.

First, select the paragraph, with your mouse by clicking before the word "water" and dragging your mouse across the paragraph toward the word "surface" in the same paragraph.

Then click the "Cut" icon in the Clipboard group of the HOME tab.

Enter a space after the image.

Then click the "Paste" icon in the Clipboard group of the HOME tab.

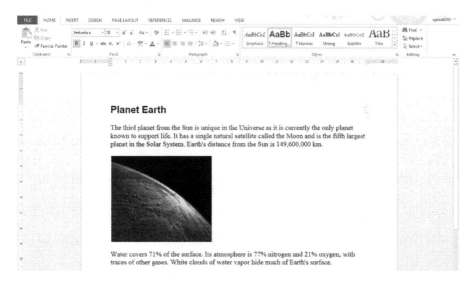

Follow the same method for copy. Remember, though, the copy command makes a copy of the original paragraph, rather than removing it.

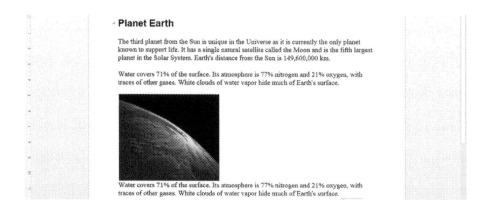

Adding Images

Adding images to your document is easy. There are two types.

- Your own photos and pictures.

- Clipart. This is a large library of images that can be used in your documents.

The easiest way to add your own photographs or pictures is to find them in your File Explorer window and drag them on top of your document.

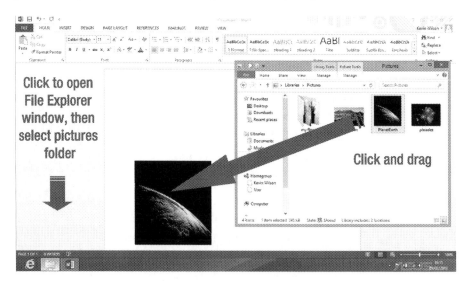

It helps to position your windows as shown above.

You might need to resize the image. To do this, click on the image, and you'll see small handles appear on each corner of the image. These are called resize handles and you can use them by clicking and dragging a corner toward the center of the image to make it smaller, as shown below.

Water covers 71% of the surface. Its atmosphere is 77% nitrogen and 21% oxygen, with traces of other gases. White clouds of water vapor hide much of Earth's surface.

Rotate handle.
Click and drag left
and right to spin
your image around

Resize handle.

Resize handle.
Click and drag to change
size of photo

Cropping Images

To crop an image, first drag and drop an image from your "Pictures" library into your document, as shown in the following screen.

Click on the image and click the FORMAT tab. From the FORMAT tab, click the "Crop" icon in the Size group.

If you look closely at your image, you will see crop handles around the edges of the image.

Click and drag these around the part of the image you want.

The dark grey portions will be removed to leave only the image inside the crop square.

Adding Clipart

To insert clipart, go to your INSERT tab, and click the "Online Pictures" icon in the Illustrations group.

Then type in what you are looking for in the dialog box.

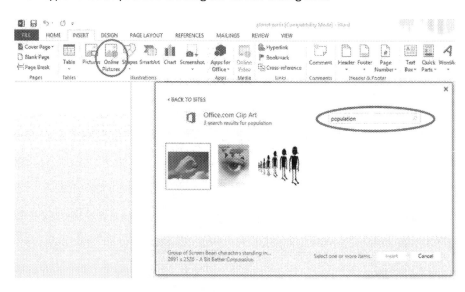

Double-click the picture you want to insert.

World Population

The human population of the world is estimated by the United States Census Bureau to be 6,821,600,000. The world population has been growing continuously since the end of the Black Death around 1400.

Formatting Images

When you click on your image, another tab called PICTURE TOOLS FORMAT appears.

This allows you to add effects and lay out your pictures on your page.

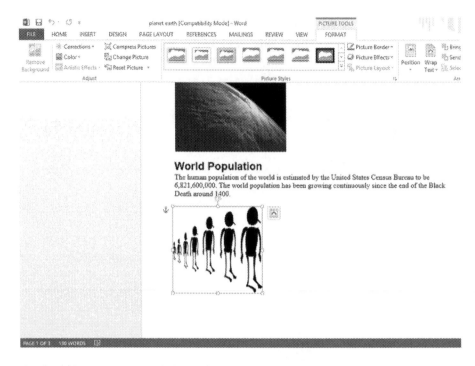

The first thing we want to do is change the text wrapping. Text wrapping enables you to surround a picture or diagram with text.

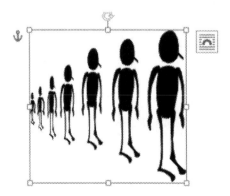

Click on your image, and go to the PICTURE TOOLS FORMAT tab.

Go the Arrange group, and click the "Wrap Text" icon. Then select "Square" from the drop-down menu. This wraps the text squarely around the image. Do this with the photograph as well.

Now you should be able to drag and position your images into the document and have the text wrap itself neatly around the images, as shown below.

Planet Earth

The third planet from the Sun is unique in the
Universe as it is currently the only planet known to
support life. It has a single natural satellite called the
Moon and is the fifth largest planet in the Solar
System. Earth's distance from the Sun is 149,600,000
km.

Water covers 71% of the surface. Its atmosphere is
77% nitrogen and 21% oxygen, with traces of other
gases. White clouds of water vapor hide much of
Earth's surface.

World Population

The human population of the world is estimated by the United
States Census Bureau to be 6,821,600,000. The world population
has been growing continuously since the end of the Black Death
around 1400.

Adding Effects to Images

To add effects to your images, such as shadows and borders, click on your
image, and then select the PICTURE TOOLS FORMAT tab.

In this example, click on the planet earth photo. Next, click the "Picture
Effects" icon in the Picture Styles group. Select "Shadow" from the drop-
down list. Then select an "Outer" shadow, as shown below.

Do this with both images; try a different picture effect on the second image. Perhaps a nice reflection effect.

Adding Tables

To insert a table, make sure you click in your document where you want the table to appear. In this example, I want it to appear just below the world population paragraph.

World Population

The human population of the world is estimated by the United States Census Bureau to be 6,821,600,000. The world population has been growing continuously since the end of the Black Death around 1400.

Go to your INSERT tab and select the "Table" icon from the Tables group. In the grid that appears, highlight the number of rows and columns you want. For this table, I chose one row and two columns.

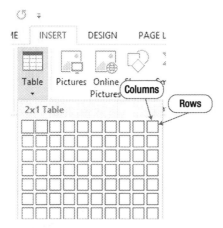

This will add a table with one row and two columns to your document.

World Population

The human population of the world is estimated by the United States Census Bureau to be 6,821,600,000. The world population has been growing continuously since the end of the Black Death around 1400.

When working with tables, two new tabs appear, TABLE TOOLS DESIGN and TABLE TOOLS LAYOUT.

The TABLE TOOLS DESIGN tab allows you to select preset designs for your table, such as column and row shading, borders, and more.

For this table, I am going to choose one with black headings and gray shaded rows.

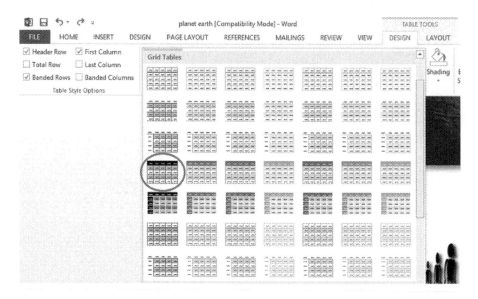

You can now enter the data into your table and Word will shade and format the table for you.

World Population

The human population of the world is estimated by the United States Census Bureau to be 6,821,600,000. The world population has been growing continuously since the end of the Black Death around 1400.

Year	Population (millions)
1960	3
1980	4
1990	5
2000	6
2030	9
2050	12

Saving Your Work

To save your work, click the small disk icon in the top left-hand corner of the screen.

In the Save As screen, you need to tell Word where you want to save the document.

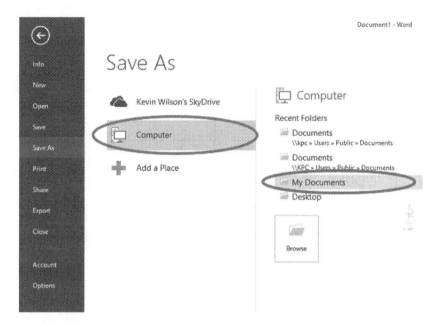

Save it into your Computer > My Documents folder, as shown above. This saves the file to your local computer.

You can also save to your SkyDrive if you want to use Office 365's sharing features, so you can access your work from anywhere.

Next, Word will ask you what you want to call the file. Think of a meaningful name describing the work. In this case, "planet earth."

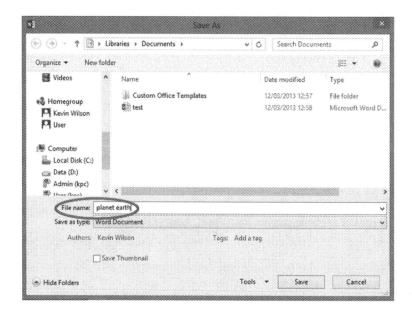

Click the "Save" button.

Printing Your Work

To print your document, click the FILE tab on the top left-hand corner of the screen.

In the following screen, select the correct printer and number of copies you want.

Finally, click the big "Print" icon.

CHAPTER 4

■ ■ ■

Microsoft PowerPoint 2013

Microsoft PowerPoint allows you to create multimedia presentations.

Starting PowerPoint

To launch PowerPoint, go to the Start screen and select "PowerPoint 2013."

After PowerPoint has loaded, select one of the following templates to start a new presentation or select "Blank Presentation" to start your own. I'm going to go with the "Mesh" template. Your most recently saved presentations are shown in the orange pane on the left-hand side of the screen.

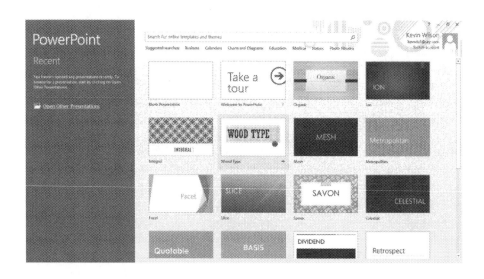

Following is PowerPoint's main screen. The tools are grouped into tabs, according to their function.

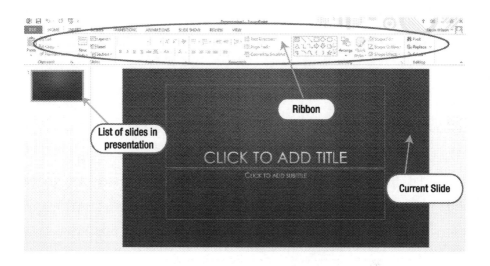

The Ribbon

In PowerPoint, the tools on the Ribbon are arranged in tabs according to their use.

The HOME Tab

The HOME tab is where you will find all the tools to do with text formatting, such as making text bold, changing fonts, or changing the color of the text. These are your most commonly used tools.

The INSERT Tab

This is where you will find all the tools to do with inserting photos, graphics, tables, charts, sounds, movies, and more.

The DESIGN Tab

This is where you will find all the tools to do with the look of your slide, such as the slide background and various themes that are available for quick formatting.

The TRANSITIONS Tab

This is where you will find all the tools that add effects as slides transition from one to the next.

The ANIMATIONS Tab

This is where you will find all the tools to add various animations to slides.

The SLIDESHOW Tab

This is where you will find all the tools to do with setting up your slideshow and running your presentation.

Designing a Slide

In PowerPoint, you can add photos, clipart, charts, diagrams, text, video, sound, and animations to a slide. To better understand the process, let's walk through a quick project.

Adding a Photo to a Slide

Start by changing the arrangement of the objects on the following slide. You might notice that the image is on top of the text box.

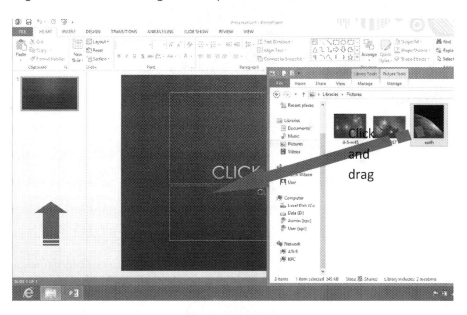

We need to bring the text box to the front, so click the title text box and on your HOME tab, in the Drawing group, click the "Arrange" icon. Then choose "Bring to Front," as shown in the following screen.

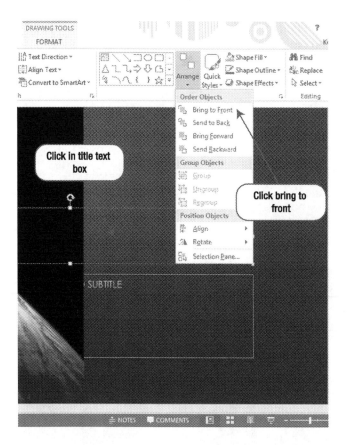

You can now add an appropriate title in the title text box; in this case, "PLANET EARTH."

PowerPoint constructs slides in layers. This means that images, text, and other elements are placed one on top of each other, as illustrated here.

These items, all arranged in layers, create the slide. Here you see the completed slide.

Resizing Images

You can resize an image to fill the whole slide by clicking on the image and dragging the resize handles to the edge of the slide.

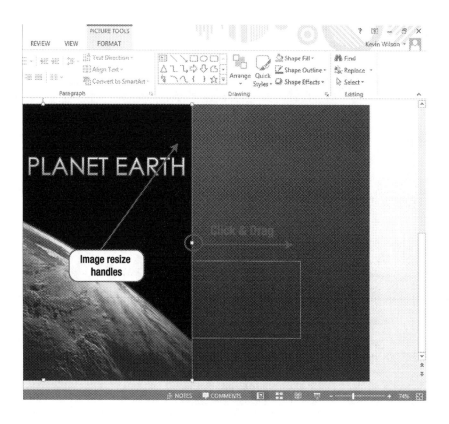

Adding a New Slide

On the HOME tab, in the Slides group, click the "New Slide" icon. Choose "Title and Content" from the resulting options.

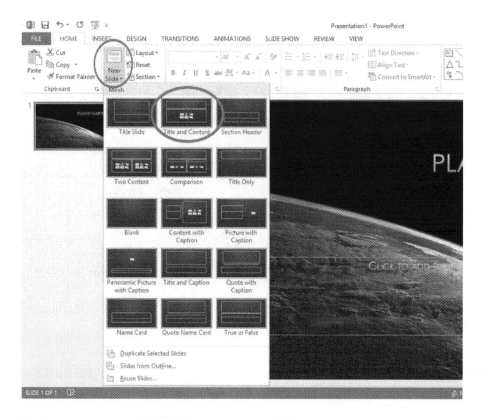

In the next screen, click "CLICK TO ADD TITLE."

Then type the title "COMMON FACTS."

Next, click "Click to add text."

Add the text in the following slide.

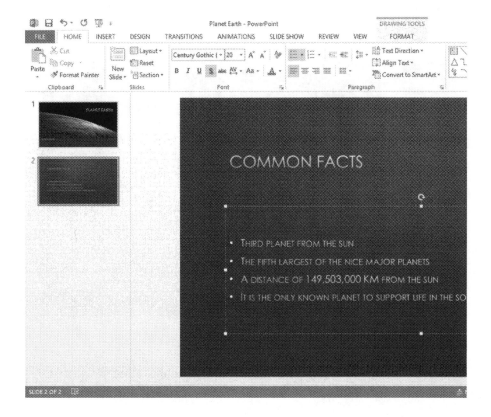

Cropping Images

Add the planet earth image again to the slide by dragging and dropping it from your "Pictures" library to your slide, as shown in the next screen.

Click the image you want to crop. A new tab will appear along the top of your screen called PICTURE TOOLS FORMAT. From the Size group, click the "Crop" icon.

Click and drag the crop handles so the crop border is around the part of the image you want to keep.

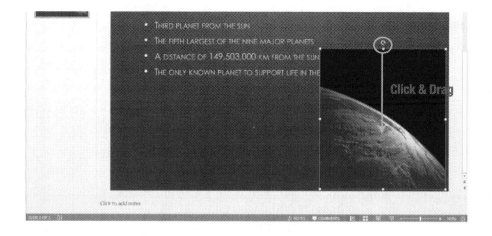

You can then position your image where you want it in your slide. In this example, I have moved it to the bottom.

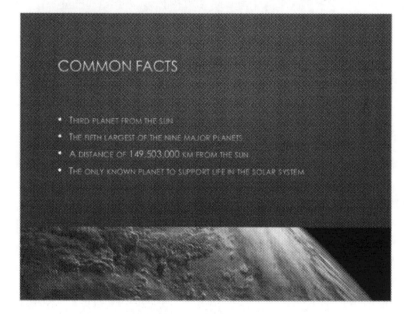

Adding Special Effects

Slide transitions and slide animations are two special effects that will enhance your presentation.

73

Slide Transitions

A slide transition is an animation or effect that is displayed when you move from one slide to the next.

To add transitions to PowerPoint slides, you need to go to the TRANSITIONS tab. On the left-hand pane, click the slide you want to add, and then click one of the transition effects from the "Transition to This Slide" group. In the following scree, "None" is selected.

Slide Animations

To demonstrate simple slide animations, we will create a slide in which bullet points appear one at a time instead of all at once. First, select the ANIMATIONS tab from the Quick Access Toolbar. Next, click on the text box containing the bullet points.

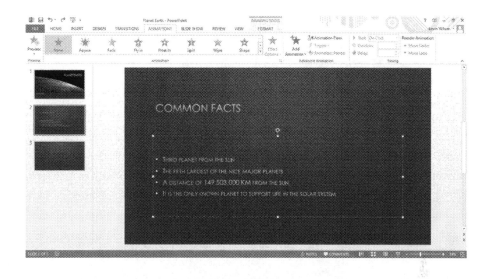

From the Animation group, click the "Appear" icon. This tells PowerPoint you want the points to appear one at a time. You can change how you want them to appear by clicking the "Effect Options" icon.

To view your presentation, press the F5 key on the keyboard.

Press Enter or click your mouse to advance a slide.

Inserting a Table

From the INSERT tab, click the "Table" icon. A drop-down menu containing a grid of squares will appear. Hover the mouse over the grid to select the number of columns and rows you want in your table.

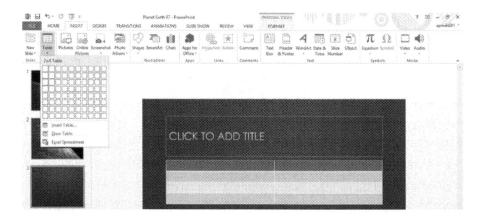

Click a cell in the table to insert the table, and then add your text to the cells.

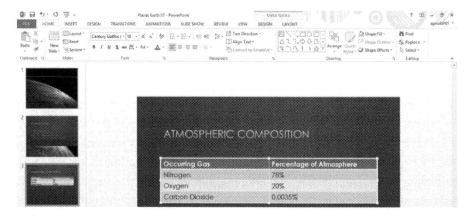

You can also format your table using PowerPoint's predesigned templates. Make sure your table is selected and click the DESIGN tab at the top of your screen. This will open a special TABLE TOOLS DESIGN tab. From here, select one of the templates.

Adding a Chart

From the INSERT tab, in the Illustrations group, click the "Chart" icon. Select a category from the left pane and review the charts that appear in the right pane. Select "Pie" for this example, and click the "OK" button.

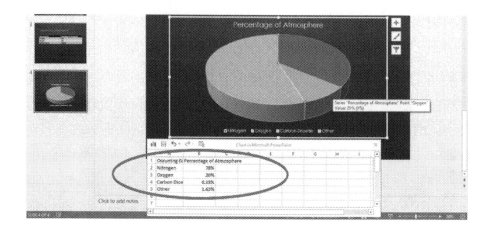

Saving Your Work

To save your work, click the small disk icon in the top left-hand corner of the screen.

In the Save As screen, choose where you want to save the document. In this case, I have chosen the Computer > My Documents folder, as shown in the following screen.

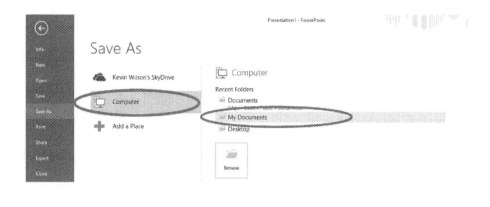

Note   You can also save to your SkyDrive if you want to use Office 365's sharing features, so you can access your work from anywhere.

PowerPoint will ask you what you want to call the file. Think of a meaningful name describing the work. In this case, "planet earth."

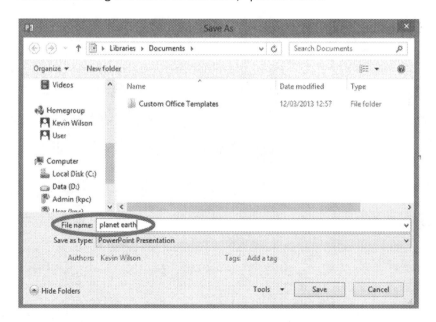

Finally, click the "Save" button.

Printing Your Work

To print your document, go to the FILE tab on the top left-hand corner of the screen.

Select the correct printer and number of copies you want, as shown in the following screen.

Then select how you want the presentation to print out. Click where it says "Full Page Slides."

This allows you to arrange more than one slide per page, and includes space to write notes. This is useful if you are giving a copy of your slides to your audience, so they can follow your presentation as you speak and take notes.

A good rule of thumb is to print three slides per page, with writing space next to each, as shown here.

Following is a print preview of what it looks like. Click the "Print" icon to print your presentation.

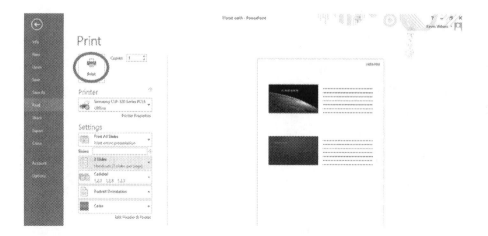

Giving Presentations

When giving your presentations, you will likely use a projector and a laptop.

Setting Up

It's best to make sure both your laptop and projector are turned off before you start.

If the projector cable has a VGA connector, then you will need the adapter.

Plug one end of the adapter into the laptop as shown in the next image. It can be inserted only one way.

Plug the other end of the adapter into the projector.

If you are using our projector, plug the other end of the projector cable into the "VGA in" port on the back of the projector.

The "VGA in" port is where the cable from the laptop plugs into; it is usually color-coded dark blue. On some projectors it's called "Computer in."

If you are using a ceiling-mounted projector in a classroom or boardroom, you don't usually have to worry about plugging in the cable on the projector.

Plug in the power and press ON/STANDBY on the projector.

Make sure the correct input is selected; on most modern projectors, this is automatic. If not, there is usually a button on the projector labeled "Input" or "Source," as shown in the following image. Press repeatedly until the computer is displayed on the projector screen.

Tip   Switch on the projector first, and then turn on the laptop. This allows the laptop to automatically detect the projector.

On most laptops, there is a function key to press if you are not getting any signal. Press and hold FN while pressing F8 (sometimes F5, depending on the model of laptop). The key will have CRT/LCD or a picture of a screen.

And that's all there is to it. You are now ready to give your presentation.

CHAPTER 5

Microsoft Excel 2013

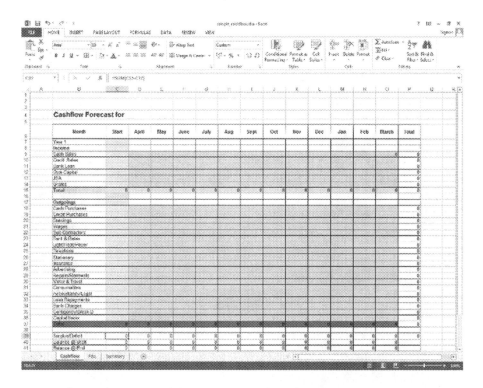

Microsoft Excel is a spreadsheet program that allows you to store, organize, and analyze information.

Starting Excel

To launch Excel, go to the Start screen and select "Excel 2013."

After Excel has loaded, click the File tab and select "New."

Select "Blank workbook" under the available templates. It will be highlighted by default.

A new, blank workbook appears in the Excel window.

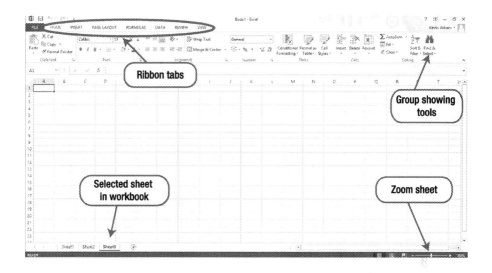

What Is a Spreadsheet?

A spreadsheet is made up of cells, each identified by a reference.

You can also select multiple cells at the same time. A group of cells is called a cell range.

You can refer to a cell range using the cell reference of the first cell and the last cell in the range, separated by a colon. For example, in the following screen, the cell range would be A1:D12.

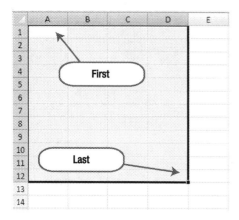

The Ribbon

All the tools used in Microsoft Excel are organized on the Ribbon into various tabs, loosely based on their function.

The most used tabs are, HOME, INSERT, PAGE LAYOUT, FORMULAS, and VIEW. For normal use of Excel, these are the ones you will be using the most.

The HOME Tab

This is where you will find your most used tools, such as basic text formatting, cell borders, cell formatting for text or numbers or currency, and much more.

The INSERT Tab

This is where you will find all your objects you can insert into your spreadsheet, such as shapes, tables, and charts.

The PAGE LAYOUT Tab

This is where you will find your page-formatting functions, such as size of paper, paper orientation when printed, page margins, and more.

The FORMULAS Tab

This is where you will find your formulas, functions, and your data-manipulation tools, such as sum functions, average, counting tools, and more.

The VIEW Tab

This is where you will find your view layouts, where you can zoom into your spreadsheet, among other functions.

Entering Data

In this example, we are creating a basic scoring sheet.

First, we type our data into the appropriate cells on the spreadsheet.

	A	22-Apr	29-Apr	06-May	13-May	20-May	27-May	03-Jun	10-Jun	17-Jun	24-Jun	01-Jul	08-Jul
2	Barbara	21	19	21	21	12	21	13	21	9	11	21	18
3	Ann	10	21	8	21	5	21	10	21	18	21	6	19
4	Flo	7	7		8		18	6	4		17	12	12
5	Emily		0	1		21	21	20	9		11		
6	Josie	21	21	6		7	12	4		3		12	7
7	Lin									4		9	4
8	Joan	19			16	12	0			15	14	15	15
9	Eva	21	14	21	18	21			5		10		21

Inserting Rows and Columns

To insert a new row between the "Flo" and "Emily" rows, right-click with your mouse on the "Emily" row; in this case, row 5.

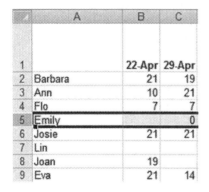

From the menu, click "Insert."

This inserts a blank row as the new row 5.

		22-Apr	29-Apr
1			
2	Barbara	21	19
3	Ann	10	21
4	Flo	7	7
5			
6	Emily		0
7	Josie	21	21
8	Lin		
9	Joan	19	
10	Eva	21	14

Resizing Rows and Columns

Resize a column or row by clicking and dragging the column or row divider lines.

Double-click on these lines to automatically size the row or column to the data that is in the cell.

Using Formulas

Using formulas allows you to perform some calculations on the data you have entered. You can add (total), multiply, subtract, find averages, or plot charts of lists of data, all depending on what your spreadsheet is analyzing.

Adding a Formula to One Row

For example, to add all the scores in my score sheet, I could add another column called "Total" and include a formula to add up the scores for the two weeks the players played.

To do this, I need to find the cell references for Barbara's scores. Her scores are in row 2 and columns B and C.

So the cell references are B2 for her score of 21, and C2 for her score of 19. All formulas begin with an equal sign (=), so in this case the formula is =B2+C2.

The result is shown in the next figure.

		22-Apr	29-Apr	Total
2	Barbara	21	19	40
3	Ann	10	21	
4	Flo	7	7	
5	Rose	9	12	
6	Emily		0	
7	Josie	21	21	
8	Lin			
9	Joan	19		
10	Eva	21	14	

Adding a Formula to Muliple Rows

You can replicate this formula for the rest of the players without having to type it in multiple times.

On the selected cell, there is a small square on the bottom right-hand side, as shown here.

Click on this and drag it with your mouse down the rest of the column.

Excel will automatically copy the formula and calculate the rest of the totals for you.

		22-Apr	29-Apr	Total
2	Barbara	21	19	40
3	Ann	10	21	31
4	Flo	7	7	14
5	Rose	9	12	21
6	Emily		0	0
7	Josie	21	21	42
8	Lin			0
9	Joan	19		19
10	Eva	21	14	35

Using Functions

A function is a predefined formula. Excel provides over 300 different functions, all designed to make analyzing your data easier. We will start with some basic, everyday functions.

Let's say we wanted to add up the number of games played automatically. We could do this with a function.

First, we need to insert a new column after the "29-Apr" column. Right-click on the column, and from the menu, click "Insert."

Call the column "Played," as shown in the following image.

	22-Apr	29-Apr	Played	Total
Barbara	21	19		40
Ann	10	21		31
Flo	7	7		14
Rose	9	12		21
Emily		0		0
Josie	21	21		42
Lin				0
Joan	19			19
Eva	21	14		35

From the FILE tab, click "Insert Function."

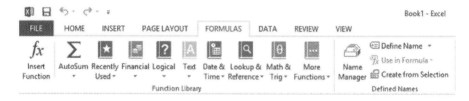

In the Insert Function dialog box, select the "COUNT" function from the list, and then click the "OK" button.

Now we need to tell the COUNT function what we want it to count. We want to count the number of games played. Barbara's scores are in cells B1 and C1, so highlight these two by dragging your mouse over, as circled in the following image.

Click the "OK" button. You can see she has played two games.

	A	B	C	D	E
1		22-Apr	29-Apr	Played	Total
2	Barbara	21	19	2	40
3	Ann	10	21		31
4	Flo	7	7		14
5	Rose	9	12		21
6	Emily		0		0
7	Josie	21	21		42
8	Lin				0
9	Joan	19			19
10	Eva	21	14		35

Replicating the Formula

Now replicate the formula. Click and drag the small square on the bottom right-hand side of the cell. Drag it down over the rest of the columns.

1		22-Apr	29-Apr	Played	Total
2	Barbara	21	19	2	40
3	Ann	10	21		31
4	Flo	7	7		14
5	Rose	9	12		21
6	Emily		0	Click & Drag	
7	Josie	21	21		
8	Lin				0
9	Joan	19			19
10	Eva	21	14		35

As shown here, Excel has automatically calculated the totals.

1		22-Apr	29-Apr	Played	Total
2	Barbara	21	19	2	40
3	Ann	10	21	2	31
4	Flo	7	7	2	14
5	Rose	9	12	2	21
6	Emily		0	1	0
7	Josie	21	21	2	42
8	Lin			0	0
9	Joan	19		1	19
10	Eva	21	14	2	35

Formatting Data

In Excel, there are different types of data to consider, such as numbers, currencies, and text.

In the next two sections, we'll format data according to numbers and currencies.

Averaging Numbers

In this example, we are going to work out the average scores over the number of games the players have played. Let's review how now.

First, insert another column and call it "Average," as shown here.

	22-Apr	29-Apr	Played	Total	Average
Barbara	21	19	2	40	
Ann	10	21	2	31	
Flo	7	7	2	14	
Rose	9	12	2	21	
Emily			0	1	0
Josie	21	21	2	42	
Lin			0	0	
Joan	19		1	19	
Eva	21	14	2	35	

In this case, the formula would be total number of games played divided by total score. To create this formula, we will use the following symbols:

Multiply	*
Divide	/
Add	+
Subtract	-

Use the forward slash for divide (/), as shown in the next image.

	A	B	C	D	E	F
1		22-Apr	29-Apr	Played	Total	Average
2	Barbara	21	19	2	40	=E2/D2
3	Ann	10	21	2	31	
4	Flo	7	7	2	14	
5	Rose	9	12	2	21	
6	Emily		0	1	0	
7	Josie	21	21	2	42	
8	Lin			0	0	
9	Joan	19		1	19	
10	Eva	21	14	2	35	

Unfortunately, the number format isn't as accurate as we want it. We need to tell Excel that the data in this column is a number accurate to two decimal places.

First, click and drag over the column of numbers to highlight it.

On the HOME tab, go to the Number format group, and click the drop-down menu to show your formatting choices.

From the drop-down menu, click "Number," as shown here.

Recording Fees

It would be the same procedure if we were, for example, recording the fees paid by the players.

Insert another column and call it "Fee." Say the fees are 9 British pounds. When we enter 9 into the column, Excel thinks it's just a number, so we need to tell Excel that it is currency.

	22-Apr	29-Apr	Played	Total	Average	Fee
Barbara	21	19	2	40	20.00	9
Ann	10	21	2	31	15.50	9
Flo	7	7	2	14	7.00	9
Rose	9	12	2	21	10.50	9
Emily		0	1	0	0.00	9
Josie	21	21	2	42	21.00	9
Lin			0	0	#DIV/0!	9
Joan	19		1	19	19.00	9
Eva	21	14	2	35	17.50	9

Select all the data in the "Fee" cell. Go back to the HOME tab, and click the drop-down arrow in the Number group to select the Number format.

This time, select "Currency" from the drop-down menu.

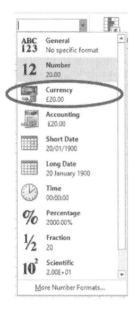

This will format all the numbers as a currency.

	22-Apr	29-Apr	Played	Total	Average	Fee
Barbara	21	19	2	40	20.00	£9.00
Ann	10	21	2	31	15.50	£9.00
Flo	7	7	2	14	7.00	£9.00
Rose	9	12	2	21	10.50	£9.00
Emily		0	1	0	0.00	£9.00
Josie	21	21	2	42	21.00	£9.00
Lin			0	0	#DIV/0!	£9.00
Joan	19		1	19	19.00	£9.00
Eva	21	14	2	35	17.50	£9.00

Adding a Chart

The easiest way to add a chart is to select from your spreadsheet a column you want for the x axis and a column you want for the y axis.

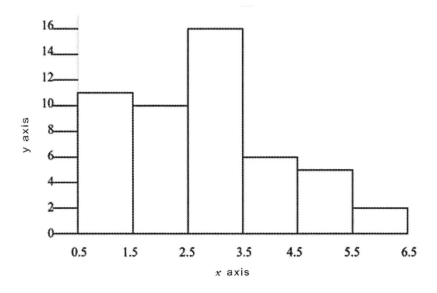

Let's create a chart for the total scores. First, select all the names in the first column. This will be the x axis on the chart.

Now hold down the Ctrl key on your keyboard. This allows you to multi-select. While holding Ctrl, select the data in the "Total" column. This will be the y axis on the chart. Note that the data in the names column is still highlighted.

E1		:	×	✓	f_x	Total		
	A	B	C	D	E			
						Click & Drag		
1		22-Apr	29-Apr	Played	Total	Average	Fee	
2	Barbara	21	19	2	40	20.00	£9.00	
3	Ann	10	21	2	31	15.50	£9.00	
4	Flo	7	7	2	14	7.00	£9.00	
5	Rose	9	12	2	21	10.50	£9.00	
6	Emily		0	1	0	0.00	£9.00	
7	Josie	21	21	2	42	21.00	£9.00	
8	Lin			0	0	#DIV/0!	£9.00	
9	Joan	19		1	19	19.00	£9.00	
10	Eva	21	14	2	35	17.50	£9.00	
11								

Release the Ctrl key and go to the INSERT tab. In the center of the tab, you will find some different types of charts, including line charts, column charts, and pie charts. Let's choose a 3D column chart, so click on the 3D column icon.

You are automatically taken to the design tab where you can select a style to auto-format the chart for you. Select a style that looks good; for example, a shaded effect.

Saving Your Work

To save your work, click the small disk icon in the top left-hand corner of the screen.

In the Save As screen, choose where you want to save the document. Save it to the Computer > My Documents folder, as shown in the following image.

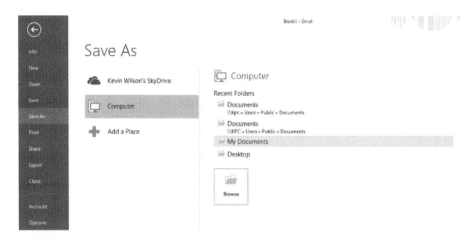

You can also save to your SkyDrive if you want to use Office 365's sharing features, so you can access your work from anywhere.

Next, Excel will ask you what you want to call the file. Think of a meaningful name describing the work. In this case, "score sheet 2013 season."

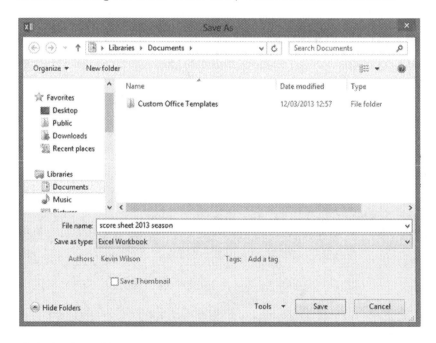

Click the "Save" button.

Printing Your Work

To print your document, click the FILE tab on the top left-hand corner of the screen.

In the following screen, select the correct printer and number of copies you want.

Finally, click the big "Print" icon button.

■ ■ ■

CHAPTER 6

Microsoft Outlook 2013

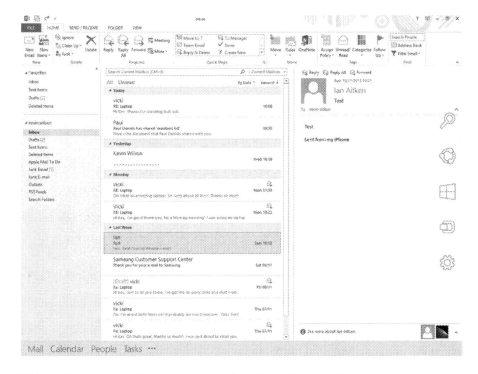

Microsoft Outlook allows you to send and receive e-mail, record appointments using the calendar feature, maintain your contacts in address books, and much more.

Setting Up Outlook

When you first start the Outlook application, you will be asked to enter your e-mail address, password, and possibly your mail settings.

On the Welcome screen, click the "Next" button, then select the "Yes" option to the question "Do you want to set up Outlook to connect to an email account?" Then click the "Next" button to continue.

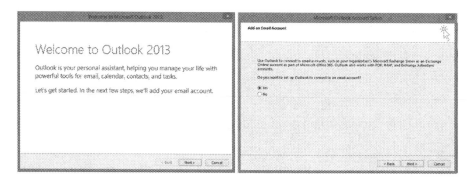

On the resulting Add Account screen, enter your name, e-mail address, and password for your Office 365 account. Then click the "Next" button to continue.

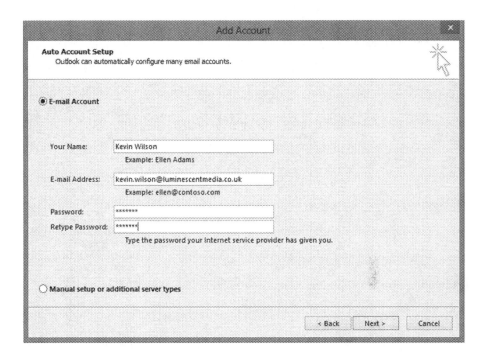

Microsoft Outlook will locate the e-mail address you have supplied and enter all the server and mail settings for you.

Getting Started with Outlook

When you start Outlook, you will see the following main screen. I've highlighted the main features you need to know in order to get started quickly and easily.

The Ribbon

All the main features and functions of Outlook are organized on the Ribbon into various tabs.

The FILE Tab

This is where you can find all your print, save, export, and account settings.

The HOME Tab

This is where you will find all your most used features, such as composing new e-mails, reply, and delete functions.

The SEND/RECEIVE Tab

This is where you will find all your functions for manual sending and receiving of e-mail. Most of the time, you won't need to use these, except when you want to manually send or receive new e-mails.

The FOLDER Tab

The FOLDER tab is where you will find functions to create folders for organizing your e-mails. For example, perhaps you would want a folder for "Vicki" to house all e-mails from Vicki, or a folder for "Accounts" for all e-mails from your accounting or banking services.

The VIEW Tab

The VIEW tab allows you to sort your e-mails by name or date, and allows you to turn on or off different sections, such as the reading pane.

Sending E-mail

From the HOME tab, in the New group, click the "New Email" icon.

In the window that appears, enter the e-mail address of your recipient in the "To" field. When you start typing in the address, Outlook will search your contacts and display suggested addresses.

You can also add e-mail addressed by clicking the "To" field and selecting the recipients from your address book. Note that you may select more than one if you want to send the same message to other people.

The "Cc" field stands for carbon copies and is used to send a copy of the message to other people.

The "Bcc" field stands for blind carbon copies. This works like the Cc field, except the recipient can't see the addresses of the other people the message has been sent to.

After you have filled out the necessary fields, type your message at the bottom.

You can also send attachments, such as photos or documents. To do this, click on the "Attach File" icon that looks like a paper clip. Select your file from the resulting Insert File dialog box, and click the "Insert" button. You can select more than one file by holding down the Ctrl key on your keyboard, as shown in the following screen on the right.

Once you are happy with your message, click the "Send" button.

Organizing Your E-mails with Rules

Rules can save you a lot of time by automatically moving messages as they arrive. For example, if you always move e-mails from a certain person to a certain folder, you could create a rule to do this automatically. You can create rules that look for a specific sender, recipient, subject, or specific words that are contained in the body of the e-mail.

Creating a New Rule

From the HOME tab, in the Move group, select the "Rules" icon.

Select "Manage Rules & Alerts..." from the drop-down menu.

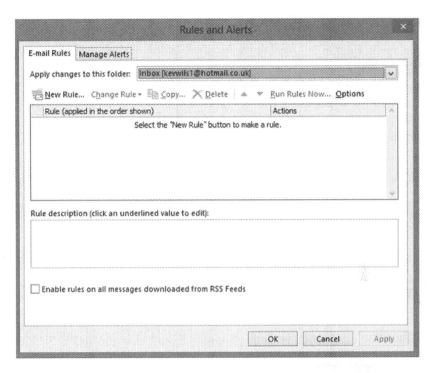

From the Rules and Alerts dialog box, click the "New Rule..." option. This will bring up the Rules Wizard. To automatically move messages that come in from a certain person, click "Move messages from someone to a folder." Then click the "Next" button.

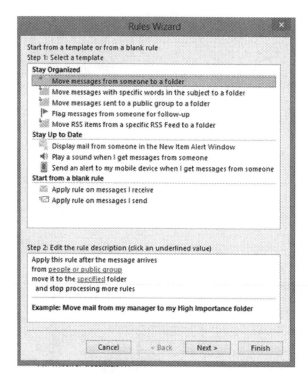

To move messages from someone, select "from people or public group" in Step 1.

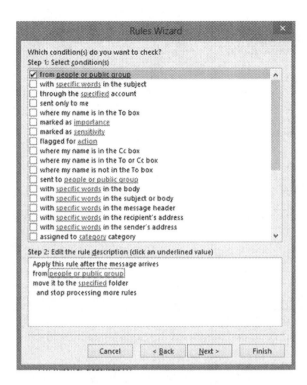

Select the e-mail address and click the "From ->" button. Then click the "OK" button.

You will then be brought back the Rules Wizard. Now, in Step 2, click "move it to the specified folder" option. In the next screen, click the "New…" button to create a new folder. In the dialog box that appears, type in the name of your folder and select "Inbox" to create the new folder in your inbox.

After you are done, click the "OK" button. All e-mails received from that e-mail address will be automatically placed in this folder. This can be very useful if you have e-mail from a lot of people.

Getting Started with the Calendar

To start the Calendar, click the calendar icon located at the bottom left of your main Outlook screen.

Once you are in your calendar, you can see how it is set up with months and dates. It is personal preference, but I find it easier to work within month view. To do this, go to the HOME tab, and within the Arrange group, click on the "Month" icon, as shown in the following screen. The quickest way to add an event or appointment is to double-click the day.

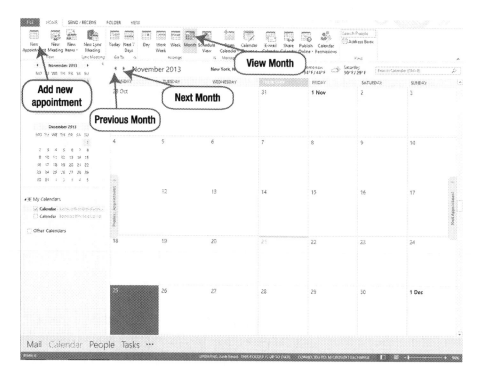

So, for example, if you wanted to add an appointment on the 25th, double-click on the 25 square.

This would bring up the following dialog box. Remove the check mark from "All day event" to allow you to enter a specific start time and end time.

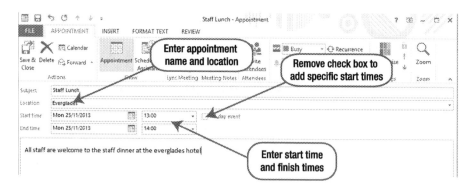

In the following calendar, you can see the appointment has been added.

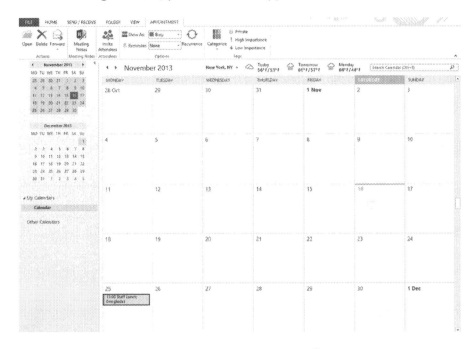

Get the eBook for only $10!

Now you can take the weightless companion with you anywhere, anytime. Your purchase of this book entitles you to 3 electronic versions for only $10.

This Apress title will prove so indispensible that you'll want to carry it with you everywhere, which is why we are offering the eBook in 3 formats for only $10 if you have already purchased the print book.

Convenient and fully searchable, the PDF version enables you to easily find and copy code—or perform examples by quickly toggling between instructions and applications. The MOBI format is ideal for your Kindle, while the ePUB can be utilized on a variety of mobile devices.

Go to www.apress.com/promo/tendollars to purchase your companion eBook.